D0407944

Pet Owner's Guide to the
CAVALIER
KING CHARLES SPANIEL

Ken Town

RINGPRESS

Published by Ringpress Books Limited,
PO Box 8, Lydney, Gloucestershire
GL15 6YD, United Kingdom.

First Published 1997
© 1997 Ringpress Books Limited.
All rights reserved

ISBN 1 86054 011 2

Printed in Hong Kong through Printworks Int. Ltd.

Contents

About the author

Ken Town has had Cavalier King Charles Spaniels for over twenty-five years. He has bred and made up two Champions, including winning Best In Show at the Cavalier King Charles Spaniel Club of Great Britain Championship Show from an entry of over 700 dogs. He shows, breeds and judges the breed, and has travelled to Sweden, Finland, the USA, Australia and New Zealand to judge at Championship shows. Ken runs a boarding kennels where many of the visitors are Cavaliers.

FACING PAGE: The Cavalier King Charles Spaniel has been adopted as a family favourite worldwide.

Photography: Carol Ann Johnson.

Chapter One

ORIGINS OF THE CAVALIER

EARLY TOY SPANIELS

The earliest information available to us concerning toy spaniels of the type now known as Cavalier King Charles Spaniels can be found in paintings of the 16th and 17th centuries. Cavaliers have always been a favourite with the aristocracy, and numerous paintings from this period show little spaniels accompanying groups of children, sitting on ladies' knees, and tucked into corners of pictures depicting family life in the Royal Courts of Europe.

ROYAL CONNECTIONS

A portrait of Henrietta of Orleans, sister of Charles II, by Mignard in 1665 shows her with a blenheim coloured spaniel, with large dark eyes, a flat skull and sweet expression, sitting on her lap. It was probably Henrietta who introduced Charles II to these little dogs who were eventually to carry his name. Charles was so taken by these spaniels that he decreed that "they be allowed in any public place" and the Royal Party was seldom seen without them.

John Evelyn, diarist of Charles II, records: "He took delight in having a number of little spaniels follow him and lie in his bed chamber".

Recently, in an attempt to test the special privilege bestowed on the pets of Charles II, a journalist approached the Palace of Westminster accompanied by a Cavalier King Charles Spaniel and claimed the right to enter along with his dog. Officials politely refused to allow them in, pointing out that the only dogs allowed inside the Palace were Guide Dogs for the Blind!

Mary Queen of Scots is known to have been devoted to her toy spaniel pet, and it is rumoured that the little dog was hiding among her skirts at the time of her execution.

During the 19th century, the Dukes of Marlborough bred red-and-white toy spaniels at Blenheim Palace, and these were firm favourites with the ladies. It is a well-known story that Sarah, Duchess of Marlborough, had a spaniel pet who gave her much comfort while her husband was away at war. In her anxiety, she is reputed to have pressed her thumb repeatedly on the spaniel's head while waiting for news of her husband. When this bitch subsequently had puppies they all bore the 'thumbprint' marking on their heads. This 'lozenge' or 'spot' is a much-sought-after feature in the breed today.

Queen Victoria was well-known for her love of animals, but the favourite of her many pets is reputed to have been 'Dash', a lovely tricolour spaniel. Paintings by Sir Edwin Landseer, commissioned by Queen Victoria and now in the collection of Her Majesty the Queen, show Dash with large, round eyes, an almost flat skull and of a similar type to many tricolours seen at the present time.

Another well-known and delightful painting by Landseer is to be found in the Tate Gallery Collection in London. It is called the *Cavaliers Pets*. It was painted in 1845 and shows a blenheim, with a perfect spot, and a tricolour lying down side by side. Most of the major art galleries in European cities whose collections contain paintings from the 17th century onwards have Cavaliers depicted as family pets, and a visit to an art gallery can often be turned into a "hunt the Cavalier" contest for children or adults.

Dash and *Cavaliers Pets* are widely reproduced in the form of miniatures or postcards, and, along with the Staffordshire figures known as 'Wally Dogs' which became so popular in Victorian times, can be found on the mantlepiece of many a Cavalier owner.

FASHION FOR SHORT FACES
With the reign of William and Mary, short-faced breeds like the Pug became popular, and it became fashionable for toy spaniels to be bred with shorter and shorter noses until they began to resemble Pekingese. These short-nosed dogs are what we now know as 'King Charles Spaniels', and they are far fewer in number than Cavaliers.

In 1886 the Toy Spaniel Club was formed and the following colours were designated: black and tans were called King Charles, tricolours (black, tan and white) were Prince Charles or King Charles I Spaniels, tan and whites were blenheims, and all-red with no white markings were known as rubies. These colours were applied to the short-nosed King Charles Spaniels, although the same colours occur in each of the two breeds. In Cavaliers today the term 'blenheim' is still used to describe tan and white, and ruby refers to all-red dogs, but 'tricolour' and 'black and tan' have superseded the other earlier names.

CRUFTS DOG SHOW 1926
The fashion for the short-nosed type lasted until 1926 when a major development took place in the creation of the Cavalier as we know it today.

An American gentleman, Roswell Eldridge, was concerned that toy spaniels with longer noses could no longer be found. The committee of Crufts Dog Show allowed him to put the following announcement in the 1926 Catalogue:

"Blenheim Spaniels of the Old Type, as shown in pictures of Charles II's time, long face, no stop, flat skull, not inclined to be domed, with spot in centre of skull. The first prize of £25 in classes 947 and 948 are given by Roswell Eldridge Esq., of New York, USA. Prizes go to the nearest to type required

The announcement appeared with a reproduction of Landseer's *Cavaliers Pets*.

Prior to this development, in 1924, the Chow Chow breeder Mrs Hewitt

ABOVE: The Duke of Marlborough and family, with a blenheim spaniel (19th century).

FACING PAGE (TOP):The King Charles Spaniel is distinguished from the Cavalier by its short face, and by its smaller size.   Photo: Ken Town.

BELOW: The Cavalier King Charles Spaniel has now become the most popular of the toy spaniel breeds.

Pitt bought a blenheim King Charles Spaniel bitch as a present for her mother. When she took the bitch, named Waif Julia, to Miss Brunne, of the Hentzau King Charles Spaniels, in order to be mated, it was suggested that the bitch would be suitable to enter in the class sponsored by Roswell Eldridge. Waif Julia duly appeared in the class, which she won, along with the £25 prize.

Mrs Hewitt Pitt then embarked on a project to breed back to the original type of longer-nosed spaniels. She had wide experience of dog breeding; her father had helped to establish Bassett Hounds in Britain around 1880. Her kennel-name Ttiweh (Hewitt reversed) is found in the pedigrees of all Cavaliers in the world today.

In 1978, Mrs Hewitt Pitt attended the Golden Jubilee Show of the Cavalier King Charles Spaniel Club and saw the fruits of all her hard work with the large entry of Cavaliers exhibited that day. She died in December of that year.

DRAWING UP THE BREED STANDARD

In 1928 the Cavalier King Charles Spaniel Club was formed at Crufts Dog Show. The secretary was Mrs Hewitt Pitt, and the Chairman was Miss Mostyn Walker, owner of Ann's Son, a blenheim dog who won the prize for best male at Crufts in the classes sponsored by Roswell Eldridge in the years 1928, 1929 and 1930. In 1936 he staged a comeback in his ninth year to win Best of Breed yet again.

At the inaugural meeting of the Cavalier Club at Crufts, the name 'Cavalier King Charles Spaniel' was chosen to differentiate the breed from its shorter-nosed cousin, and the task of drawing up a Breed Standard – the blueprint for the breed – was undertaken. The committee produced as many pictures of Toy Spaniels through the ages as could be found and placed them on the table, along with Ann's Son, who was used as a live model. The Breed Standard was formulated; points were allocated to the various desired features of the breed totalling 100 in all. Great attention was paid to the head and no fewer than 55 points were allocated to its various parts, eyes, ears, skull etc., although it was specified that under 'General Appearance and Soundness' dogs should be "active, sporting and fearless".

DEVELOPMENTS IN THE BREED

Over the years, breeders used the long-nosed throw-outs from the Charlie breeders to try and establish the correct type of head with the soft, melting expression so desired in the Cavalier. Experiments were tried crossing Cavaliers with Papillons to get the longer nose required, and it is known that some of today's dogs can trace their pedigrees back to crosses with Cocker Spaniels. The gene pool was fairly small, and the same few dogs appeared several times in the pedigrees of the early Cavaliers, particularly Ann's Son. In the early years, there were no classes for Cavaliers at dog shows and they had to appear in classes open to breeds not provided with proper classification. The breed did not have Championship status, and so most serious breeders took little notice of this obscure breed.

THE FIRST CAVALIER CHAMPION

Thanks to the determination and perseverance of the early breeders, the breed achieved official Kennel Club recognition in 1945 and the following year the first Challenge Certificates were allocated. On August 29th 1946, the first Championship Show was held at the School of Drama, Alverston, Stratford-on -Avon. The best dog at that show was Daywell Roger, and he became the breed's first Champion. He was also a highly successful stud dog, siring eleven Champion offspring, whose progeny went on to be a great influence on the breed.

The Breed Standard was revised around this time and the original points system, which had placed so much emphasis on the head, was discontinued. The General Appearance section of the new Standard required dogs to be: "active, graceful and well-balanced, absolutely fearless and sporting in character, very gay, and free from trimming and all artificial colouring."

From the early days, when the breeders of the 1920s struggled to have their dogs recognised, Cavaliers have grown tremendously in popularity, both as a show dog and as a companion dog. Cavaliers are to be found all over the world, all descended from the dogs bred by those early pioneering breeders. The success of the breed owes much to the dedication of those determined to re-establish the longer-nosed spaniel, but, in the main, it is because of the Cavalier's great charm, which has won over the hearts of so many devoted admirers.

LEFT: Taking on a puppy is a big responsibility.

BELOW: The sweet-natured Cavalier adapts well to family life.

FACING PAGE: Cavaliers enjoy each other's company, and, as far as the owner is concerned, keeping a couple of dogs does not create much more work.

Chapter Two

CHOOSING A PUPPY

FIRST CONSIDERATIONS

Before you set about the task of finding a puppy, be sure to think about the implications of adding an extra 'person' to your household and whether you really have the time and dedication required to look after it properly. Everyone in the family needs to be enthusiastic about taking on a puppy, and while children are often keen to take on responsibility at the outset, an adult must be prepared to take charge when the novelty wears off.

Is the Cavalier the right breed for you? This active Toy dog is often recommended as an ideal companion because it is so adaptable, and will fit in with a great variety of domestic situations. Whether you live on a farm in the open countryside or in an apartment in the middle of town, the Cavalier can be equally at home. So long as he has the opportunity for free

range exercise twice a day and almost constant company, he will be quite content. If you like going for long walks, a Cavalier will relish the exercise, but if you can only manage a couple of visits to the local park, this will be sufficient for his needs. Cavaliers thrive on a change of scene, and a chance to explore new surroundings, and the sight of a lead is always greeted by a wildly wagging tail.

Companionship is very important to a Cavalier. Solitude simply does not appeal, particularly in his early years, so do not embark on the project of obtaining a puppy if your lifestyle requires him to be shut up on his own for long periods. This situation usually results in a very miserable little dog who develops bad habits, such as chewing the furniture and carpets or constant barking, something that should never arise if he has company.

It is worth thinking about the possibility of having a second dog, as two Cavaliers cause very little more work than one, and the two will enjoy chasing each other about and having fun together.

THE CAVALIER CHARACTER
The Cavalier is a sweet-natured, gentle, small dog with a lively but dignified disposition. His willingness to comply with your requirements comes easily, and apart from the odd occasion when the smell of a rabbit is so intoxicating that he fails to notice your desire to put his lead on and go home, his normal behaviour shows a real joy in co-operating, with aggression playing no part in his social repertoire. The Cavalier is very vigilant and will react to unusual sights or

sounds by barking, but this rarely takes the form of confrontational behaviour.

A Cavalier's favourite place will be sitting on your lap; he is a most affectionate dog who loves everyone. Naturally exuberant, the Cavalier is especially happy with children and will join in all sorts of games. Canine visitors are always made welcome, and Cavaliers will also get on well with cats and other domestic pets, once the initial curiosity has been overcome.

It is most unusual for Cavaliers to be jealous or possessive over tidbits, and although they are often quite greedy they accept quite happily the distribution of biscuits or treats among the group.

PHYSICAL CHARACTERISTICS
The Cavalier is compact in size, usually weighing up to about 18 lb, so he will fit easily into any home, and on any lap. The coat, which can be quite profuse, does need regular grooming to keep it in good condition. Although the ears are long, it is unusual for Cavaliers to have any associated problems which can be a nuisance in some spaniel breeds. Fortunately, the Cavalier has few health problems and, provided he comes from a healthy family, visits to the vet should mainly be confined to updating the annual booster injection and having a check-up.

COLOUR
In Cavaliers, there are four colours to choose from. Most people are drawn to one particular colour because they have met a dog of this colour and liked it, or have been told by a friend that "tricolours are more intelligent"

or "rubies have the loveliest eyes". In fact, all the four colours have similar characteristics, although some lines may have certain family traits.

BLENHEIMS (tan and white): These are the most numerous, and they are usually the easiest to obtain simply because there are more blenheim bitches producing puppies than any of the three other colours. The lozenge or spot marking – the small, round marking on the top of the head – is most often found in the blenheims. Markings which are not symmetrical or excessive freckling on the face may be penalised in the show ring.

TRICOLOURS: These dogs have black markings on a white background with tan eyebrows and cheeks, and some tan under the tail, inside the ears and where the black meets the white at the tops of the legs. Absence of tan in any of these places would be penalised in the show ring. Some tricolours have almost completely black bodies with just a small amount of white on the face and legs. This would count against them in the show ring but they still make lovely pets and, in fact, some of the early tricolour champions were very heavily marked. The lozenge, or spot marking, can also occur in tricolours.

RUBIES: Ruby Cavaliers are a rich, red colour all over.

BLACK AND TANS: This colour is all-black with bright tan marking over the eyes, on the cheeks, inside the ears, on the chest, the legs and under the tail. Cavaliers of this colour are comparatively few in number and are more difficult to obtain. Rubies and black and tans are sometimes referred to as wholecolours due to the absence of white markings, and sometimes an otherwise good specimen will not be suitable as a show prospect because of a tiny patch of white on the chest, on the face or on feet, and will therefore be offered for sale as a pet.

MALE OR FEMALE
The next important choice is whether to have a male or a female puppy. The first consideration is whether having a bitch in season will cause any problems. It is usual for a bitch to come in season twice a year, starting with the first season at any time from six months of age. The bitch normally keeps herself very clean, and so the main concern would be whether unwelcome suitors would be a problem. If you intend to breed a litter, then, of course, a female would be your choice.

Males are equally suitable as family pets as females. Males are just as affectionate; they do not come in season, and they are rarely aggressive. The males mature into very handsome adults since the coat and feathering in a male tends to be slightly more profuse and glamorous than that of a bitch.

FINDING A BREEDER
The best course of action is to contact your national Kennel Club, who will put you in touch with a Breed Club secretary in your area. The secretary will have a list of breeders, and may even know who has a litter available. Be patient, as Cavaliers are very popular and it may take a little time to obtain a suitable puppy. A reputable breeder will be only too pleased to show you his or her stock, as long as you make an appointment. If you see the mother of the litter and other

CAVALIER COLOURS

LEFT: The blenheim (tan and white) Cavalier is the most numerous, and, therefore, the easiest to obtain.

BELOW: The tricoloured Cavalier has black markings on a white background, with tan on the eyebrows and cheeks.

ABOVE: The ruby Cavalier is a rich, red colour, with no markings.

BELOW: The black and tan Cavalier has a black coat with tan markings.

close relatives, this will give you an idea of how the puppies will develop. Remember that a nursing bitch will not be in the peak of condition, and she will probably be looking less glamorous than she normally would. The coat usually goes into a heavy moult shortly after a litter, and some bitches put so much effort into rearing their families that it is at the expense of their own condition.

ASSESSING THE PUPPIES

If there are several puppies available that are the sex and colour of your choice, it will be a matter of picking out the puppy that most appeals to you. Bear in mind that, even at this tender age, the energetic, boisterous puppy will probably retain these tendencies as he grows up, and the very quiet, timid puppy will do likewise. Ideally you should be able to find an alert, curious, plump, playful puppy, who seems to take to you and shows signs of an affectionate nature.

With all four colours, the tan markings will be much paler at the eight week stage; they will deepen in colour as the dog matures. The paleness is particularly noticeable with blenheims and rubies. The colour of the mother's coat may give you a guide as to how the colour will turn out. The texture of a puppy's coat is rather fluffy and fine. This will change at about five months when the sleeker, shinier adult coat begins to come through.

Umbilical hernias occur from time to time, and this small lump on the tummy, where the cord was originally attached to the afterbirth, does not usually cause any problem. Your vet may wish to remove it at a later stage

if it is necessary to do some other operation which requires an anaesthetic.

Ask the breeder if the puppies' parents have had their hearts and eyes tested, and whether any defects were found. Some Cavaliers may develop heart murmurs at about six years of age. Fortunately, in most cases, the dog continues to live a happy, healthy life without medication up to eleven years of age or more. Quite a few live to fourteen years old and some even longer. Ask the breeder what sort of life span can be expected from his line.

The breeder will also want to find out a lot of information about you as prospective new owners of one of his precious puppies. The responsible breeder needs to be confident that you can provide the puppy with the proper care and attention required throughout its life, and most will want an assurance that you will return the dog should unforeseen circumstances arise which mean that you can no longer provide an adequate home.

The genuine breeder will be happy to explain why any or all of the puppies offered to you are not suitable as show prospects. In most cases, this will be due to markings or some cosmetic detail that would be penalised in the show ring. If your preference is for a male, it is worth asking if he has two apparently normal testicles as, if not, surgery may be required at a later stage.

PREPARING YOUR HOME

Before your puppy arrives, check that your house and garden are puppy-proof. An eight-week-old Cavalier puppy will be able to wriggle through or under any fence that is not perfectly secure. If you have previously had a dog, or you already own one, you may well find that a curious puppy will not be confined by fencing that is sufficient for a mature dog. For instance, chicken wire soon becomes rusty or damaged, and it is easy to push underneath it. It is advisable to place concrete paving slabs, or some similar hard surface, along the bottom of the fence, as this will prevent the puppy digging underneath.

An open gate is an invitation for a puppy to venture into the exciting world beyond, so a self-closing device and a catch which secures the gate automatically on closing would be a wise precaution.

Screening your garden from neighbours with shrubs or solid timber may help prevent the puppy from becoming too noisy, as he may well be inclined to bark at the arrogant cat who knows he cannot be 'got at' and chooses to bask in the sun in full view! The approaching postman or paper boy may well provoke an outburst of barking, as the puppy announces that this is his territory and warns you of the appearance of an 'invader'.

In the house, it is important that electric wire leads and similar dangerous items are not left in easy reach, as chewing these can have serious consequences. Rubbish-bins have a great fascination for young puppies on account of all the interesting smells they contain, and these, along with plastic bags, should be kept out of reach or behind a closed cupboard door.

BUYING EQUIPMENT
BEDS AND BEDDING
CARDBOARD BOX: A strong cardboard box, with all sides covered and a hole cut in the front for access, makes a practical and cosy bed for the first few weeks. It does not matter if this gets chewed or damaged, and as the puppy becomes more civilised it can be replaced by a permanent bed. Some pieces of blanket or old woollen garments will allow the puppy to make a cosy nest and, being enclosed, he will be out of any draughts. The bits of blankets etc. can be discarded and replaced by the sheepskin-like, synthetic bedding material. This has a tough backing so that it lies flat. Puppies seldom do much damage by chewing it, and it is easily washed and dried. It is unlikely that your puppy will urinate on his bedding, but if he does, the moisture passes through the dense pile, keeping it dry.

WICKER BASKETS: These used to be very popular, but it is now generally thought that the disadvantages outweigh the advantages. Wicker is easily chewed, and the sharp projections make it hazardous for dog and owner alike. Wicker baskets are also difficult to clean, as dust and germs can lurk in the crevices.

PLASTIC BEDS: The oval-shaped, plastic beds are highly recommended. These beds are easy to clean, with no corners to trap the dust, and a piece of oval-shaped fleece bedding will provide a warm, comfortable sleeping surface. An oval, plastic bed, measuring 21 inches across the base, is about the right size for a Cavalier.

The puppy you choose should be clean, with bright eyes, and a lively, inquisitive manner.

If you are looking for a show puppy, the breeder will help you to assess important breed points.

ABOVE: You will need to buy a food bowl and a drinking bowl. Stainless-steel food bowls are long-lasting and easy to clean; a heavy, earthenware bowl is ideal for water.

Photo: Ken Town.

RIGHT: A nylon or leather collar and lead is suitable for a Cavalier.

BEAN-BAGS: These are very popular with Cavaliers. The polystyrene beans reflect the body heat, and their mobility allows the bed to contour around the dog's body shape. The outer cover can be un-zipped and removed for washing. The one disadvantage is that the beans sometimes leak, especially if the puppy has a nibble, and zips can be an attractive target for trying out newly-emerging teeth. The same problem also applies to dog duvets, which can look very attractive with their stylish fabric covers.

INDOOR KENNELS: This is now considered a standard item of equipment among many dog owners. It provides a safe haven for the puppy, and it also speeds up the process of house-training, as a dog is reluctant to foul his own bed. They can also be used for travelling, and this means that you have a familiar 'home' for your dog when you are staying away. An indoor kennel or crate is easy to clean and the fleece bedding can be used inside it. Feeding the puppy inside an indoor kennel helps get him used to it, and this also removes any distractions which may take his mind off his food. However, it would be quite wrong to leave your puppy shut up in an indoor kennel for long periods. An indoor kennel must never be used as a punishment; the puppy must always *want* to go into his crate.

PUPPY PEN: This is a useful acquisition, as it means your puppy can be confined to a specific area some of the time until he has learnt more about house-training.

BOWLS
You will need to provide a water dish that cannot be knocked over too easily, or be picked up and carried about in your puppy's mouth. It is worth investing in a heavy, earthenware spaniel bowl for this purpose. The sides of this type of bowl taper towards the top to prevent the ears from dipping into the water when the dog is drinking. For feeding, I prefer to use stainless-steel bowls, as they are more hygienic and not as likely to be chewed as plastic bowls. These should be washed after each meal as the fly population will find the residues (should there be any) an attractive place to lay eggs, and deposit bacteria in the process. Don't forget, dogs can get food poisoning as well as humans.

COLLARS
Start off with a soft collar, which can easily be adjusted as the puppy's neck grows. Your puppy will soon get used to the feel of this, particularly if you have a game with him to distract his attention. In most countries, dogs are required by law to wear a collar, bearing means of identification. The best kind of collar for permanent use is one made of rolled leather, with an attachment for an identity disc and another attachment to which a lead can be fastened. An adult Cavalier's neck is about thirteen inches in circumference, so you will need a collar which can be adjusted to within an inch or so either way, ensuring that when fastened it will not pull over the ears.

Metal choke-chains are not suitable for a Cavalier. They damage the coat, and a properly-trained Cavalier does not require such heavy-handed treatment. An all-in-one slip collar and lead, which is mostly nylon with a chain loop attached to the collar, gives a milder checking action, and this is often used in the show ring.

LEADS

I use a nylon lead, which is approximately 3/8th of an inch wide and 42 inches long, attached to a slip collar. Leather or nylon leads are equally suitable, and it is very much a matter of personal preference for the individual owner. Metal chain leads are not recommended for the Cavalier, neither is the harness. It should never be necessary to resort to the halter-like device, which goes over the muzzle, that some large, strong and difficult dogs need for their owners to remain in control.

Keep an eye on the lead-clip, as wear and tear sometimes make this unsafe and you do not want to discover it has come undone at a crucial moment. A nylon lead with a ring at the end is a useful item in an emergency. The end of the lead can be slipped through the ring to make a makeshift slip-lead.

COLLECTING THE PUPPY

Arrange a mutually convenient time to collect the puppy so that he has time to settle into his new surroundings and familiarise himself with his new family before being sent to bed in a strange place for the first time. The breeder will give you details of the diet the puppy is used to and may give you a small supply to last until you are able to obtain some for yourself. This prevents any problems with an upset tummy due to change of diet. Details of worming treatment should be given

as well as advice on grooming, exercise and general care. You should be given a copy of your puppy's pedigree, a receipt for the purchase price, and the Kennel Club registration certificate with change of ownership forms.

On the way home, assuming you are travelling by car, a responsible adult should be entrusted with holding the puppy, with a towel for him to sit on, and some tissues readily available in case of accidents.

ARRIVING HOME

When you arrive home, give your puppy a chance to explore, and then introduce him to his new bed. Remember that although it is all very exciting to have this lovely new puppy in the house, he will get tired, and after playing for a while, he will need to sleep. Do not worry if your puppy is not interested in his food to begin with. He may well be too excited to settle down and eat, but he will soon make up for lost time! Supervise introductions with all members of the family, and if you have other animals, make sure the puppy is not left alone with them until they have established a peaceable relationship.

THE FIRST NIGHT

There are two schools of thought about how to settle the puppy down for the night for the first time. The first is to start as you mean to go on and at bedtime, after your puppy has been taken outside to relieve himself, put the puppy to bed with a biscuit and/or toy, shut the kitchen door and hope he settles down when everyone goes off to bed. Some puppies will be fine, and after a whimper or two will decide it is nice to have the chance of

ABOVE: Remember that your puppy will chew, so it is advisable to start off with a cardboard box for a first bed.

LEFT: A tough, plastic bed is suitable for both puppy and adult dog.

Photo: Ken Town.

RIGHT:
Many owners find a crate an invaluable item of equipment.

BELOW:
Make sure your puppy has his own toys to play with. These should be chew-resistant in order to avoid potential accidents.

a good sleep after an eventful day, and will curl up and be quite content until daylight next morning. A covered hot-water bottle may be a comfort, replacing the warmth of his litter mates who are no longer around, and a slight noise, such as the ticking of a clock or a radio left on very quietly, may provide the reassurance the puppy needs when he is left alone for the first time. Going back to see your pup when he starts crying may be counter-productive, as he will quickly realise that this sort of behaviour results in the reappearance of his new human friends.

The second school of thought is to use a high-sided cardboard box or pet carrier, and keep the puppy in your bedroom, so that you are on hand with a reassuring word or cuddle to ease him gently into his new lifestyle. This does not need to be a long term measure, and after a night or two when the puppy has become used to his bed and new surroundings, he will probably settle down in the kitchen, knowing that you are not far away.

HEALTH CHECKS

Many breeders have puppies checked by their own vet, and some have the first injection of the vaccination programme given prior to going to their new homes. In any event, it is advisable to visit to your own vet within a few days of acquiring a new puppy. The puppy can be given a general check-up, and the inoculation programme can be arranged. The age at which vets start the vaccination programme varies from one area to another. The vaccinations will protect your puppy from killer diseases, such as parvovirus, distemper, leptospirosis, and canine hepatitis.

Chapter Three

CARING FOR YOUR CAVALIER

FEEDING

There are numerous options when it comes to choosing food for dogs, and the choice can be quite bewildering. However, the most important factor is to provide a balanced diet which contains all the vitamins and minerals the puppy needs to grow and develop properly. Unlike humans, dogs will eat the same food every day with no signs of being bored with repetition. It is often the owners who think they should provide variety, and this can sometimes result in dogs becoming 'picky' feeders, refusing to eat what is put down in the hope that a more appetising dinner will appear.

As a general guide the Cavalier puppy will require the following feeds:
8-12 weeks: 4 feeds daily
12-18 weeks: 3 feeds daily
Clean, fresh drinking water should be available at all times.

At 10-12 months you can change from puppy food to adult dog food but do make the change gradually. Cavaliers vary a lot in the amount of food they want and need. Many are very greedy and are constantly craving tidbits, others will look with disdain at a dish of food and seem to exist on very little.

DIET VARIATIONS

MILK

Most puppies at eight weeks have milk and cereal for breakfast. The cereal can be wheatflakes or a crumbled-up rusk dissolved in the milk. Cow's milk is high in lactose and, if at all possible, it is far better to use goat's milk. This is widely available in health food shops, and it can be stored in the freezer. The high lactose content of cow's milk can cause loose motions, whereas goat's milk, which is lower in lactose and higher in protein, is much closer to bitch's milk. Canned rice pudding, which most puppies love, is a convenient alternative to milk and cereal.

MEAT

It is now possible to obtain a large variety of meat from pet stores in frozen 1lb packs. Beef, chicken, fish and tripe are all easy to obtain, but they should be cooked before feeding. If you decide to use this type of meat it should be fed with about half as much puppy meal, moistened with a little warm water or stock. This type of diet, or household scraps, will need to be supplemented by a vitamin/mineral supplement. It is

The Cavalier needs a balanced diet and regular exercise in order to stay fit and healthy.

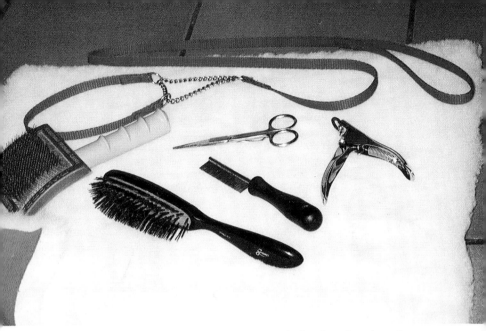

ABOVE: Selection of equipment including a slicker brush, a bristle brush, a comb, a pair of scissors, and nail-clippers.

BELOW: It is important to establish a grooming routine from an early age. Start off using a bristle brush for the body coat.

important to follow the instructions recommended by the manufacturers and only give the amounts specified. It can be just as harmful to give too much of these supplements as too little. Canned meat is now produced specifically for puppies. This has the advantage that it does not need to be cooked, and it contains the appropriate vitamins and minerals. Some canned dog food contains cereal as well as meat, so check whether you need to add puppy meal.

COMPLETE DIETS

These are now extremely popular and there are many different brands available. All the necessary vitamins and minerals are incorporated into the balanced formula, and so supplements should not be added. The amount of faeces produced by dogs on this type of food tends to be less that those on a meat and meal diet; the stools are usually firm and very easy to clean up. It is most important that dogs fed on this type of food have water freely available as the dry pellets absorb a lot of water. In comparison with a meat and meal diet the amount of complete food required seems a bit skimpy, but the dogs seem to thrive on it and when the pellets absorb water they swell up and the dogs seem quite satisfied. It is very convenient to use; it is not messy and does not attract flies. It is also very handy for travelling as the pellets can be kept in a convenient polythene container and dispensed when required.

TREATS AND SNACKS

Cavaliers love to be given a tidbit by their owner and will often eat something given by hand that would be ignored if it were in a dish. It is easy to fall into the trap of hand-feeding, as Cavaliers love the extra attention this provides. A hard biscuit, given as a treat, is good for the teeth but do not do this too often as you don't want your Cavalier to put on too much weight. I always give all the dogs a hard biscuit last thing at night before going to bed, and they then retire for the night fully contented.

THE OVERWEIGHT CAVALIER

This is a tendency in some Cavaliers to become overweight, and, in most cases, this is due to an over indulgent owner who cannot resist that pleading look when chocolates or other delicacies are being enjoyed by the family. However, succumbing to this behaviour leads to two problems. Firstly, your dog becomes a nuisance if, every time a paper rustles, he rushes over to demand his tidbit. Secondly, your dog will become overweight, and his teeth will suffer. If you cannot resist his pleas, give him a dog biscuit, which will not be so bad for his teeth or waistline.

If your dog starts to become obese, substitute half of his dinner with some cooked cabbage, chopped up finely with the rest of the food. Cabbage is mostly composed of water, and so a reduction in weight can be achieved in a short time without the dog thinking he is on starvation rations. Too much weight puts an extra burden on the heart, and Cavaliers can ill afford this extra strain. (See Chapter Seven: Health Care.)

PLANNING A DIET

A suggested diet for a puppy of eight weeks would be as follows:-

8 am	Two dessertspoonfuls of canned rice pudding with a little hot water added to make the consistency a little more liquid.
12 noon	Two ounces of chopped or canned meat with about half the volume of slightly moistened puppy meal. Add an appropriate vitamin and mineral supplement to this meal according to the manufacturers recommendations
4 pm	Half a cup of warmed goat's milk with a teaspoonful of honey and half a rusk mixed into it.
9 pm	One ounce of chopped or canned meat with the same volume of moistened puppy meal.

The puppy meal should be moistened with hot water (not boiling) or stock to make a moist, crumbly consistency which is not too wet.

An alternative diet:

8 am	Half a cup of milk or goat's milk with a teaspoonful of honey and some wheatflakes.
12 noon	Two dessertspoonfuls of complete puppy diet with a teaspoonful of cooked mince or canned meat mixed with it.
4 pm	Scrambled egg, (half a large egg will be enough so scramble the whole egg and keep the other half in the fridge until tomorrow).
9 pm	Same as noon.

There is a lot of variation in the amount of food individuals require, so be guided by common sense. If one of the meals seems to be superfluous, phase it out and re-schedule the other feeds to make the intervals between each meal approximately the same.

EXERCISE

Puppies should not be given formal exercise until their vaccination protection is complete. They should not go on pavements or places frequented by other dogs until two weeks after the final injection. Playing in the house and garden will provide all the exercise needed at this stage. By about fourteen weeks of age your puppy's immunity should be sufficient for him to have a short walk each day lasting five to ten minutes, allowing plenty of time for him to investigate new sights and smells, and to get used to being on the lead. Remember that at this tender age your puppy will tire quickly, both physically and mentally, and he will need plenty of opportunity to rest.

As your Cavalier gets bigger and stronger, the amount of exercise can be increased. However, he should not have really strenuous exercise until he is 9-10 months of age, when the joints and limbs will be sufficiently mature to allow this with no ill effects.

The adult Cavalier will enjoy as

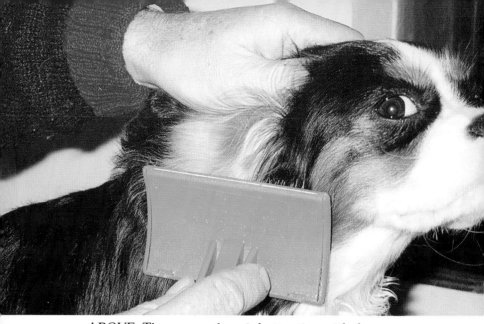

ABOVE: The ears need special attention with the slicker-brush as this is where mats and tangles can form.   *Photo: Ken Town.*

BELOW: After brushing, a fine-toothed comb can be used on the feathering.

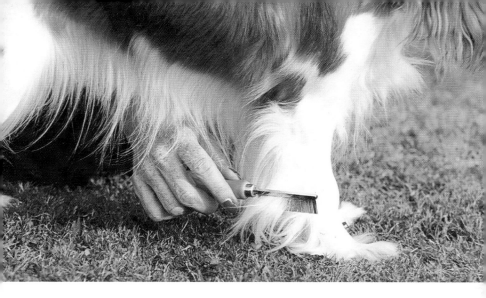

ABOVE: The long hair on the legs will need to be combed.

RIGHT: Gentle handling when grooming sensitive areas will be appreciated.

much exercise as the average owner will be able to provide. A brisk half-hour walk once a day will keep the muscles firm, and free range exercise several times a week will not only be physically beneficial but will do a lot for his mental condition, allowing him to let off steam and work off any frustrations. This is another occasion when keeping a second Cavalier is a great boon. If you only have one dog, it may be possible to meet up regularly with another Cavalier owner to enable the dogs to enjoy the fun and games only possible with a like-minded playmate.

Cavaliers are not aggressive dogs, and they will seldom want to involve themselves in any anti-social behaviour with the other doggy visitors to parks and public exercise areas. They are more likely to roll over on their backs in a gesture of submission. However, it is important that you are in control of your dog at all times, and anticipate any problems that may arise with other dogs.

A cross-country ramble will be a great treat for your Cavalier, but beware of crops which may have been sprayed, and ensure you have control of your dog should farm animals be in the vicinity. There are beauty spots and public footpaths where the local authority still allows dogs access, with the proviso that owners clean up after their pets, and this rule should be respected. Cavaliers also love a run on the beach, and some of them are quite keen to go in the water. Have regard for other people on the beach, as not everyone will appreciate a wet, sandy Cavalier jumping up at them. It is only by adopting an attitude of consideration for the non dog-owning public that we will be able to preserve the opportunities to let our dogs run free.

GROOMING AND BATHING

The adult Cavalier has a beautiful, soft, shining coat, as long as a sensible grooming routine is maintained. This does not need to take very long; if it is done every day about ten minutes is all that is required. If you keep to a regular routine, the coat will not get matted and the dog will enjoy his daily tidy-up. If you neglect little tangles, particularly those that form behind the ears and around the hindquarters, the job will become more difficult and will become an ordeal for dog and owner alike.

It is a good idea to get your puppy used to the daily tidy-up from an early age. He will enjoy the attention, and it will also get him used to being handled. This is valuable training for any dog, and it is essential if you plan to show your Cavalier. At first the coat is fairly short, with no substantial feathering, so a gentle brushing will not upset your puppy. If he gets used to the routine, and you train him to accept it sensibly, when the coat grows longer and needs more thorough attention, he should take this in his stride.

It is important to stand your puppy on a firm surface that will not wobble, so that he does not feel insecure. The ideal surface is a sturdy table or work top, with a rubber-backed bath mat, car mat, or piece of carpet for your puppy to stand on. For the first few occasions, make it more of a social occasion, with plenty of stroking and encouragement. On no account leave the puppy alone or he may jump off the table and hurt himself; so if the phone rings, put puppy back on the floor again before you answer it!

At this stage all you will need is a brush and some damp tissues. A bristle-brush is the best type to use. Your puppy will be most interested in the brush, especially as you start to stroke it through the coat. Discourage him from biting at it, and try to persuade him to stand still and not fidget too much. Talk to your puppy, and carry on grooming until he accepts the feel of the brush. If he struggles, try to persevere. If a puppy succeeds in discouraging you from your objective, he will have scored a 'victory,' and it will become more difficult to get him to accept the procedure as he gets older. When you feel you have achieved enough with the brush, give his eyes and around the mouth a wipe with some damp tissue, praise him, and give him a little tidbit. You can also spend five minutes tidying his ears in the evening, with the puppy sitting on your knee.

GROOMING EQUIPMENT
As your puppy grows bigger and the coat starts to lengthen, you will need to use additional grooming equipment. You will need:
A slicker brush: This has bent, wire bristles, to ease out any little knots.
A bristle brush: This is needed for the main job of grooming.
A fine-toothed comb: This will help to keep the coat tangle-free.
A piece of chamois leather or silk: This helps to add the finishing touches and gives the coat a nice sheen.
A pair of blunt-ended scissors: These will be useful for trimming the hair under the pads.

Nail-clippers: The guillotine type are the easiest to use.
Tissues: To wipe the eyes and around the mouth.
Canine toothpaste and a toothbrush: Regular teeth-cleaning will help reduce the build-up of tartar and will keep the gums healthy.

GROOMING ROUTINE
When your dog has a mature coat, which can be from about ten months onwards, it is necessary to follow a regular routine to keep the coat and skin in good condition. By this time, your Cavalier will be used to standing on his non-slip surface to be groomed.

Start with the slicker brush and gently brush down the neck from the top of the head, under the neck, around the chest, working from front to back until you have covered the body with the exception of the face and ears. Pay particular attention to the feathering on the legs and on the hindquarters where the hair is thickest.

When you have gone over the whole dog with the slicker brush, which will tease out any dead hair, move to the ears which will need systematic and thorough grooming. Start with the left ear and lie it along the dog's neck so the inner side is exposed. Begin with stroking the slicker brush through the first few hairs on the outside edge of the ear, and, with each stroke, take in a few more hairs until you have worked your way right across this side of the ear. Great care must be taken not to scratch the skin, which is exposed near the entrance to the ear canal.

When you have completed this side, having paid particular attention to the area just behind the ear, close to the

If the nails grow too long, they will need to be trimmed using guillotine type nail-clippers.

Puppies enjoy gnawing at rawhide chews, and this also helps to keep the teeth clean.

The Cavalier's teeth must meet in a scissor bite with the upper teeth closing over-lapping the lower.

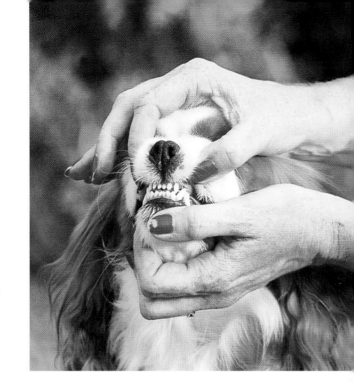

Regular brushing with a toothbrush and canine toothpaste will be of benefit to the adult Cavalier.

neck, where little tangles always start, turn the ear flap over and do exactly the same to the outer surface of the ear. Repeat this with the right ear. No matter how often you do this, you will always end up with some dead hair in the slicker brush which would otherwise be discarded on the carpet or on the furniture, so it will save you some work in the long run.

The next stage is to brush all parts thoroughly with the bristle brush. This stimulates the blood supply and helps to keep the skin in good condition. Check under the tummy to see if there are any little knots. This is a sensitive area, so treat it carefully, ensuring you leave it tidy and free of any tangles. Follow this by combing through the long hair on the ears, legs, chest and hindquarters with the fine comb. Wipe around the eyes and mouth with a damp tissue, and finish off with the dry chamois or piece of silk which will help provide a nice sheen. If you follow this procedure every day you will have a dog to be proud of. Missing the occasional day will not matter too much, but be careful you do not get out of the habit as a badly-neglected coat is quite a problem to sort out.

Modern central heating systems seem to result in dogs losing hair all the year round, rather than the twice a year moult which used to be the case. It is far better to stick to a grooming routine and remove dead hair from the dog before it makes a mess, and this will also keep him clean and healthy. The daily examination provides an opportunity to keep a close check on your dog's overall condition, and will reveal any problems such as cuts, scurf, ticks or fleas, or any bits of vegetation picked up on his walk and caught in the coat.

TEETH

The pH of a Cavalier's saliva is such that it encourages the build-up of tartar on the teeth, and this often becomes something of a problem. This can be minimised by encouraging gnawing on nylon or raw beef bones. On no account give chicken or chop bones. Specially manufactured canine toothpaste helps to reduce tartar, and this can be applied with a toothbrush or with a rubber device, which is like a thimble. This is placed on your finger, with the toothpaste smeared on to it, and you then apply it to the teeth. Most dogs like the flavour of the toothpaste, but some are not too keen on having things poked into their mouths. Again, early training will accustom your Cavalier to this routine.

When your dog is four or five years old, it may be necessary for the teeth to be descaled by the vet, and this will require an anaesthetic. The vet will probably draw your attention to this on one of the annual visits to have the vaccination booster. Hard, dry crunchy food, such as some complete diets, are less likely to allow tartar to develop than soft, moist food.

FEET AND NAILS

From time to time, it may be necessary to trim the hair under the pads which may grow too long and become matted. This can be done with blunt-ended scissors; it should be the only part of the coat where trimming of any sort is practised. If your Cavalier has plenty of exercise on hard ground, it should not be necessary to trim the nails at all. Old dogs, who do not get as much exercise, may need to have their nails clipped from time to time. If you need to do this, use a pair of guillotine type nail-clippers, which are obtainable at good pet shops. Care should be taken to cut below the quick or it will be painful and cause bleeding. If your Cavalier still has his dew claws – the nails that grow a few inches up the inside of the front legs – it will probably be necessary to trim these from time to time, as they do not get any wear to keep them short. They can sometimes grow in a circle, which can result in penetrating the skin or causing a sore.

BATHING

Dogs do not sweat through the skin like humans, so most of the deposits found in the coat are picked up externally. If your dog rolls in some obnoxious, foul-smelling substance which he may well do, tomato ketchup applied to the area and washed off will get rid of the smell. If he is kept tidy by regular grooming, as described above, he will not need to be bathed very often as dirt picked up on his walks will brush out. However, a bath will do him no harm. Many show Cavaliers have a bath every week of the show season with no ill effects.

Before bathing, give your dog a good grooming to remove as much dead hair as possible. A sink at waist height, big enough to accommodate a Cavalier is ideal, and most people find this easier than using a bath. Dog hairs can be collected before they go down the drain by placing a metal sieve-type device over the plug hole. This can be obtained from any

hardware shop. Place a rubber mat in the sink for your dog to stand on so that he feels secure and there is no risk of him slipping. An extra pair of hands from a sensible helper will be useful for the first few baths until your dog has learnt to stand quietly and calmly. This will leave both your hands free for the job in hand. A shower type spray that will disperse water at a constant temperature is the most convenient way to wet and rinse your dog, otherwise a large bowl or a bucket full of water at a lukewarm temperature will be needed. You will need a canine shampoo, towels, the bristle grooming brush and possibly a waterproof apron. Once you have bathed your dog, he will need to be dried thoroughly. Prepare everything you need in advance so that you start drying your dog as soon as you have finished bathing; a wet dog could easily become chilled.

The technique employed for bathing is fairly straightforward. I usually wet the dog all over, and then apply the shampoo to the neck, back, ears, etc. until a good lather is worked up all over the dog. After thorough rinsing, apply more shampoo and then rinse off. I always use baby shampoo for the dog's head to avoid stinging if any should enter the eyes. Care should be taken when rinsing the head to avoid the spray going into the dog's nostrils, which he will hate. With practice you will become an expert, and the dog will trust you to rinse his face by raising his head, with his eyes closed, and the spray gently rinsing the area around his muzzle. Cotton-wool placed in the ears before bathing will prevent water from entering the ear canal.

When you are bathing your Cavalier, the water should be at body temperature.

Apply shampoo to the coat. This should be a specially manufactured canine shampoo.

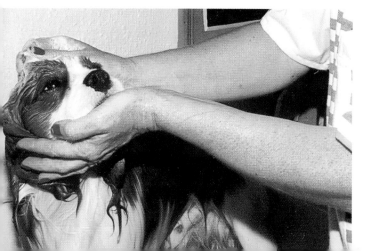

Work the shampoo into a rich lather, making sure you avoid the eyes, nose and mouth.

The coat must be thoroughly rinsed after shampooing.

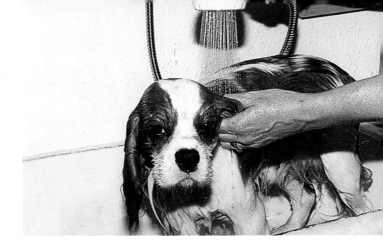

Few Cavaliers can resist a good shake after a bath!

Finish off by drying your dog with a hand-held dryer.

I use a piece of special, absorbent material, which is like an artificial chamois leather, to soak up the excess moisture from the coat before using a towel. A good rub with a dry, thick towel will then take more of the moisture out of the coat. At the first opportunity, your dog will have a good shake and if it is a dry warm day, this can be done outside.

DRYING YOUR DOG

The next step is the drying process. I stand the dog on the grooming worktop, and after an initial quick brush over, I position the dog in front of the hair-dryer and systematically work my way over the whole dog until he is completely dry. I brush each part of the coat with the bristle brush as it is blown by the warm air from the dryer. The noise the dryer makes can be a bit frightening at first so, if possible, start it on low and build up as the dog gets used to it. The ears are best dried in the same way as they are groomed. That is to lie the wet ear along the neck with the warm air from the dryer blowing along the lie of the coat, not into the ear canal. Brush gently until that side is dry, then turn the ear over and deal with the other side in the same way.

I use a dryer, specially designed for dogs, which is on its own heavy stand, and the drying end can easily be manoeuvred into various positions. Many dryers designed for human use have stands available, so if you are going to do the bathing without the help of an assistant, this may prove to be a useful acquisition. If you do not possess a hair-dryer then it would be best if you confine your dog-bathing activities to warm summer days when you can dry your dog outside in the sun. Your dog can also be dried by a warm fire, though this takes a little longer. An electric dryer helps the coat to lie flat as it dries while it is being constantly and carefully brushed. If you let your dog dry naturally outside on a warm day it may result in some curliness developing.

If you have used cotton-wool in the ears, make sure you take this out before your Cavalier settles down in his favourite spot. Make sure he is completely dry, especially if it is bedtime.

Chapter Four

TRAINING YOUR CAVALIER

During the first few weeks after the arrival of your new puppy, you should be prepared to spend a lot of time getting to know and understand each other. This is a formative period in the development of the character of your puppy, and it is important that you are on hand to notice the budding traits and channel them in the right direction.

EARLY LESSONS

The tone of voice you adopt when talking to your puppy will convey a lot, and if you speak in a sharp tone he will know you are cross with him – no matter what words you use. The word "No" will, inevitably, be one of the first your puppy will learn. Any time he embarks on a course of action which is not acceptable, such as climbing up the stairs or chewing something which is not his, the word "No", spoken in a sharp tone, will quickly make him realise that he must stop.

The rest of your command words are a matter of personal choice. "Sit" and "Stay" are useful, and "Stand" will be needed if you intend to show your dog. If you teach your puppy to respond to the word "Stay", it will be a useful aid in an emergency if you

need your dog to keep still. A prompt response to this command has saved many a dog's life, particularly if a dangerous situation occurs in traffic.

At this stage in training, take a positive line and praise enthusiastically when your puppy responds in the way you want; try to ignore other behaviour for the present. Friends will want to come and see your new pet and it will be good for him to meet new people and get used to being handled by strangers.

When the puppy has got used to his bed and come to regard it as his home, it will be a valuable lesson to leave him on his own for short periods of about ten minutes, while you and your friends go into another room. This will accustom your puppy to being left alone. When you return, give him a cheerful welcome. Hopefully, he will have spent the time you have been away playing with a toy or gnawing a rawhide chew. If he has made a fuss, do not be too sympathetic, or you will give him the impression that he only has to whimper to bring you running – and he will quickly learn to exploit that.

HOUSE-TRAINING

It will be necessary to put quite a lot

LEFT: The Cavalier is intelligent and responsive, which will make training easier.

BELOW: A well-socialised dog will adapt to a variety of situations and will lie in harmony with other dogs – regardless of how big they are!

The golden rule is to keep training sessions short, interspersing them with games.

of time and effort into house-training at first until the puppy gets the idea of what is required. He will always need to urinate as soon as he wakes, and you should anticipate this and take him outside before it happens on the kitchen floor. At first it will probably be necessary to carry him out in order to avoid accidents. Use a command such as "Be clean" to create an association between the word and the act, and praise him when he performs. Later on, as he starts getting the message, let him follow you out to the garden and make a big fuss of him if he does what is required. Do not be tempted to scold him if it does not go according to plan. It is very important that you stay with him until the deed is done so that you can use your chosen word and praise him afterwards.

Your puppy will also need to urinate and defecate after a meal, and again, you must repeat the ritual of taking him outside and staying with him until he has performed. Regardless of the weather, do not be too quick to bring him in. It is important that you supervise the puppy and are on hand to praise him when success is achieved. Remember, the fewer mistakes your puppy makes indoors, the sooner he will learn to be clean outside.

During the night it would be unreasonable to expect your puppy to last for some eight hours without having an accident. Most puppies will use newspaper if it is left down for them, but make sure you only leave it down at night, or your puppy will get confused. If your puppy has an accident, do not make an issue of it or, worse still, push his face at it. Your puppy will soon learn if you adopt the positive approach explained above. If you use an indoor kennel, you will find the process of house-training is speeded up, as he will be most reluctant to foul his bed.

With increasing public pressure against fouling by dogs in public places, it is highly desirable that your dog learns to perform his toilet duties in your own garden, where they can be cleaned up immediately.

LEAD TRAINING

I like to start puppies off with a soft, cat collar before a lead is introduced. Your puppy may well scratch at the collar at first, but he will soon get used to the feel of it. During the next few days, let him wear the collar for longer and longer periods until it can be left on all the time without bothering him. When your puppy has reached this stage, a lead can now be fastened to the collar and left trailing behind the puppy. From time to time, you should pick up the lead in order to get the puppy used to the feeling of restraint which it will cause. Do not wrestle if he pulls away, and do not do this for more than a few minutes as otherwise he will probably start chewing the trailing lead – a habit you do not wish to encourage.

After a few sessions of attaching the lead, which can be done over several days, the puppy should be encouraged to walk around the room in any direction he likes, with you holding the lead. Some forward movement is all that is required, and the lessons should be short and relaxed. Do not worry if you feel you are not making much progress. You and your puppy cannot venture into the outside world until the vaccination programme has been completed, so you have a number of weeks to work on this lesson. You may find that attracting your puppy's attention with a toy will encourage him to go forward. Another solution is to take your puppy out with another dog who is well-behaved on the lead. The puppy will be so interested in keeping up with his new friend, he will soon forget about resisting the lead.

Once your puppy is walking on the lead with free, forward movement, get him used to keeping to your left hand side. In Obedience competitions and in the show ring, the dog is required to work on the left, and even if you are confining your interest to pet-training, it is useful to adopt this practice, leaving your right hand free. I like my dogs to trot at a steady pace with no tension on the lead. At first, your puppy will probably pull and want to move too quickly. Short checks will restrain this, and this should be coupled with the command "Heel", indicating that you wish your dog to stay close to you and not meander from side to side in front of you.

Repetition and encouragement will soon produce the desired result. No matter how difficult it seems to be in the early stages, do persevere. There is nothing worse than seeing a full-grown Cavalier pulling his owner along; this is a tiresome and unnecessary way for a dog to behave. If you feel you are not making satisfactory progress yourself, seek the help of a training class where you and your puppy will meet others learning the same lessons, and an instructor will be on hand to give you advice.

SOCIALISATION

If you want your dog to be well-behaved in all situations, he must learn to mix with people, animals, and other dogs, and he must learn to be calm in traffic. The period between seven and fourteen weeks is a critical time for socialisation with humans, and it is important that the puppy does not have any traumatic experiences during this time, such as suffering from fear or acute anxiety, or it may have an effect for the rest of his life. All activities should be engineered to encourage good behaviour; there should be plenty of encouragement and praise when things go according to plan, while shortcomings should be treated with very mild disapproval. Smacking, shouting, or leaving the puppy alone for over an hour will be counter-productive.

In order that your puppy grows into a confident, well-adjusted dog, you must become the pack leader, a role which his mother would have adopted. As pack leader, you provide food, comfort, security and keep the puppy away from danger in whatever form it takes. He will look to you for support in all the new experiences he will encounter, and it will be a natural response for him to do what the pack leader wants. Try to introduce your puppy to a wide range of experiences during this period; he should meet men, women and children and, from the safety of your arms, he should hear the passing traffic and see something of the activities of street life.

At this stage, your puppy will not have the protection of vaccination, so for excursions outside he will need to be carried. If you adopt a bright and breezy attitude, it will convey the

TOP LEFT: When teaching the Sit, apply gentle pressure to the hindquarters as you give the command.

TOP RIGHT: You can use a tidbit when teaching the Down.

BELOW: The dog will follow his nose and go into the Down position. Remember to reward with plenty of praise.

ABOVE: As your Cavalier becomes more confident, you can introduce the Stay command from the Sit or the Down position.

BELOW: Gradually increase the distance you leave the dog. In time, your Cavalier will be able to perform this exercise off the lead.

message that there is nothing to worry about, even when you visit the vet for his injection. Friends with well-behaved pets should be encouraged to bring them around to meet your puppy so that he will learn to accept the presence of other dogs. As soon as the inoculation programme has been completed, you can join a training class, many of which run special classes for socialising puppies.

BASIC EXERCISES
In order that your puppy is well-behaved at all times, it will be necessary for him to learn some basic exercises. You must decide which exercises you want to teach him, and then embark on a consistent plan where reward and association are the key words. For example, should you wish your puppy to lie down on command, wait until he lies down of his own volition, and then say the word "Down" followed by praise or, perhaps, a tidbit. After a very short time, your puppy will associate the word "Down" with going into the down position, and he will realise that this reaction will be rewarded with praise or a tidbit. This is particularly successful in teaching a dog to stand, the posture he must adopt in the show ring. I always teach my dogs "Stand" when we start our daily walk routine. If something catches your dog's eye in the distance and he adopts an alert, four-square stance, I immediately seize the opportunity and say "Stand". At this stage, the action precedes the command but, no matter, the association is established, the reward follows, and eventually the dog understands what is required. Make sure you end all lessons on a good

note, and never get cross if things do not work out the way you wanted. Tidbits should be given immediately the desired act is performed, and these can be alternated with verbal praise.

Correction of misdeeds is very difficult, unless you are present at the time they are committed. It is pointless and damaging to make a fuss if you come home and reprimand your puppy for something he may have done twenty minutes previously. You may think that the guilty look on your puppy's face shows that he knows he has been naughty, but this is more likely to be a reaction to the look on your face or the tone of your voice. In reality he will be thoroughly confused, and he may start to regard your return home with fear and trepidation.

COMING WHEN CALLED
Taking a dog for a walk should be a pleasure for dog and owner alike. However, it is essential that you are in control of your dog at all times, and you must be confident that your dog will come back when called.

At eight weeks of age a puppy is much more willing to come when called than it will be at sixteen weeks or older. Take advantage of this natural tendency, and establish a habit which you can build on. Keep some tidbits in your pocket and, during the course of everyday activity, call the puppy from time to time and reward him with a tidbit and verbal praise. All too often, an owner will wait until the puppy is out for a walk and has discovered some interesting scent, and then wonder why the pup fails to return when he is called. Worse still, when the puppy does come back, he is rewarded by being scolded. It is essential that the puppy associates being called and returning to you with pleasure, whether this is in the form of a tidbit or verbal praise. If you only call him to curtail his freedom by putting him back on the lead, he will soon become disenchanted and prefer to remain free. If, when he does return, he is met by a good scolding, you will have effectively intensified the bad associations he already had on returning to you.

When your Cavalier is enjoying free range exercise, call him to you frequently, reward him with a tidbit, and then let him go off again. In this way, your puppy will associate being called and coming back to you with pleasant associations, and will soon accept that sometimes you just want a chat and a cuddle with him, and sometimes his lead will be put on. You can even practise putting the lead on for a few minutes, then letting him free again, so he realises that even if you want him under close control for a while, it might not mean the end of the walk. As always in training – think positive. The extension lead has become very popular among pet owners. This allows the dog greater freedom than a conventional lead – but the owner remains in control. Personally, I do not think that an extension lead should be used as a substitute for effective training. In fact, I have seen some tangled mix-ups between extension lead users, which, if not hilarious, can be positively dangerous.

CAR TRAVEL
My dogs love going out in the car and are never car-sick. This is because they get used to short trips in the car as young puppies, and they know that there will usually be a walk in an interesting location at the end of the journey. The puppy who is car-sick is often the one who is dumped in the back, with no regard for his comfort and security, and then taken on a trip to the vet to have an injection, which means the car has bad associations from then onwards.

A good introduction to the car is to start with short journeys of about ten minutes. If possible, your puppy should be sitting on someone's lap, who will reassure him, providing a pleasant introduction to car travel. It is a wise precaution to have a collar on the puppy which can be a means of restraint should the car door be unexpectedly opened. You may wish to designate a particular place in the car for the puppy to travel, such as the back seat or the rear part of a hatchback. In this case, place a rug for the puppy to lie on, and give the "Stay" command.

My dogs always travel in the car in a crate, and these are very effective in providing a secure, comfortable, well-ventilated refuge, where the dogs are happy to settle. The car-guard, available for many makes of car, can be effective, but a lot of Cavaliers will find a way through, under or round it, unless it is a very good fit.

If car-sickness is a persistent problem, ask your vet to prescribe a travel sickness tablet. This will usually provide a solution.

MINI-AGILITY
Mini-agility, a scaled down version of Agility, has been specially designed for smaller dogs. This is an entertaining activity involving the negotiation of

FACING PAGE (TOP): Cavaliers love competing in Mini-agility, and many have proved very successful in this discipline.

FACING PAGE (BOTTOM): Cavaliers can be trained to a high level of Obedience. Maxholt Special Love Story (Piccadilly), trained by Janet York in the USA, is an Obedience Champion, and also has Agility, Scent and Flyball titles.

Photo courtesy: Ken Town.

ABOVE: Maxholt Special Love Story completes a perfect retrieve with the dumb-bell. *Photo courtesy: Ken Town.*

numerous obstacles such as tunnels, weaving poles, see-saws, jumps, etc. It is becoming increasingly popular with the public, and a lot of Cavaliers are very good at it. Both dog and owner need to be very fit as it requires the round to be completed in a fast time. This sport should not be tackled until your Cavalier is fully grown, as it could be damaging to developing puppies. A basic grounding in Obedience is required for Mini-agility, so until your puppy is a year old, it would be best to work on the basic lessons of Obedience training until he is physically ready to cope with such a rigorous sport.

OBEDIENCE TRAINING
There are Obedience training clubs in most major towns, and enthusiasts meet weekly or bi-weekly to further their training in this discipline. Many Cavaliers have an aptitude for it, but if it is your intention to go in for this sport, choose a puppy with a very out-going attitude and an adventurous spirit. Cavaliers want to please, and this is a vital characteristic for obedience training.

The qualifications which can be achieved internationally are CD (Companion Dog), CDX (Companion Dog Excellent), UD (Utility Dog) and UDX (Utility Dog Excellent). It is quite difficult to obtain these titles in the UK as there are few concessions for small dogs and they have to compete on equal terms with the German Shepherds, Border Collies etc., whereas in the USA, obstacles are tailored to suit the size of the breed.

In the USA there is also a tracking qualification (Tracking Dog and Tracking Dog Excellent) which some Cavaliers have attained. If you intend to take up Obedience training seriously, it will be worth joining your local training class where you will benefit from the help and advice of an experienced trainer, not to mention the shared experiences of other competitors.

THERAPY DOGS
Therapy Dogs, often known as PAT dogs in the UK, are dogs which go with their owners to visit sick or elderly people in hospitals and other long-stay institutions. Your local breed club should be able to put you in touch with the appropriate organisation. Cavaliers make excellent therapy dogs as they are so friendly and affectionate, and the effect they have on patients in hospitals, old peoples homes etc. is often extremely beneficial.

The dog and owner will be expected to make regular visits to a designated hospital or nursing home in order that the patients can start to build up a relationship with a particular pet and, often, the owner too. When a patient has become introspective and withdrawn, perhaps not having any visits from people, the undemanding contact with an affectionate Cavalier can have wonderful results.

Chapter Five

SHOWING THE CAVALIER

THE SHOW WORLD

Most people, when buying their first Cavalier, are simply looking for a handsome pet who is out-going and friendly. However, if he turns out to be a good specimen of his breed, one of the proud owner's 'knowledgeable' friends may suggest taking him to a show. Be careful, this may be the first step to an expensive and compulsive hobby that could radically change your way of life! It is difficult to explain the logic of rising at 4am, driving hundreds of miles in sometimes dreadful weather conditions, spending all day in a noisy, crowded venue with nowhere comfortable to sit down, in order to exhibit your dog in a large class, with only a moderate chance of winning or even coming out of the ring with one of the five prize cards available – and then, the long drive home again, exhausted.

In spite of this, hundreds of dedicated Cavalier owners make this a way of life, and we owe them a great deal of gratitude because it is through their dedication and skill that our breed has gone from strength to strength, become well-known by the general public, and has improved enormously since the early years in terms of closeness to type and genetic soundness. Apart from breeding good-looking dogs that are capable of winning top awards, most breeders who are involved in the show scene also take great care in using stock from lines which are long-living and free from genetic problems.

There is enormous pleasure to be gained from the camaraderie that exists in the world of dog showing. It encompasses people from all walks of life, and everyone has an equal chance of being successful if they possess the necessary skills. Lifelong friendships and great social activity, sometimes covering a much broader spectrum than purely 'doggy' matters, spring up all the time.

WHAT THE JUDGE IS LOOKING FOR

In order to decide whether your Cavalier stands a chance of being successful in the show ring, you need to understand what the judge is looking for. It is the task of the judge to examine all the dogs entered, and place them in order of merit according to his interpretation of the Breed Standard. In some countries there are slight differences in the wording of the Breed Standard, but these are minor

FACING PAGE (TOP): To be successful in the show ring, your Cavalier must be a typical specimen and conform as closely as possible to the Breed Standard.   Photo: Ken Town.

FACING PAGE (BOTTOM): The kind, gentle expression of the Cavalier is a hallmark of the breed.

ABOVE: The judge will assess coat and colour, and will be looking to see if the dog has a cheerful, friendly disposition.

Photo courtesy: Ken Town.

details, and Cavaliers should appear to be very similar to each other the world over. The overall impression should be of an active, graceful dog with a well-balanced outline, and a gentle pleasing expression. He should be about the right size and have a cheerful, friendly nature and a long, silky coat. When your Cavalier moves, he should do so freely, with plenty of drive from the hind legs to push him along, his back should remain level with no humps or dips, and the tail should wag cheerfully from side to side. A well-arched neck, carrying the head proudly, does much to create a pleasing profile. A really good Cavalier head with large, dark, round eyes, softly cushioned foreface, long, well-set ears, and that melting expression, is a joy to behold and a unique feature of our lovely breed.

Most judges who specialise in judging Cavaliers consider the head to be very important, and they may be willing to overlook shortcomings in other areas if the head is particularly pleasing. Although the Cavalier is in the Toy Group, this should not imply that he is incapable of walking for miles, or is unable to perform acts of great athletic prowess – and this should be apparent in his manner in the ring. An over-exuberant puppy, who prefers fidgeting about to standing like a statue, will be preferred to one who lacks animation or looks bored and disinterested – but it is difficult to assess the balance and construction of a puppy who refuses to keep still, even for a moment.

The way a dog's bones are structured makes a considerable difference to the overall impression he creates. The length and angulation of the bones in the shoulders and hindquarters play a large part in the way the dog carries himself and moves. For example, a shoulder blade that is of a good length, and set at an angle of about 45 degrees to the vertical, is more likely to allow a well-arched neck to carry the head than a shoulder blade which is almost vertical, causing the neck to poke out forwards with the head carried low.

A bright-eyed, stylish dog will endear himself to the judge, but over-enthusiasm in tail carriage when the tail is carried very high, or, horror of horrors, in an arc over the back, will be considered a serious fault by most judges. Very long legs or a long body will not appeal to the judge, who wants to see a symmetrical, balanced outline with no exaggerations. The whole dog should give an impression of balance and cohesion with a pleasing head and expression, and a well-presented coat which has the look and feel of quality.

TYPES OF SHOW

THE UK: There are five types of show to be found in Britain at the present time and all of them are licenced by the Kennel Club. These graduate in size and status culminating in Championship Shows where Challenge Certificates are on offer to the best dog and the best bitch of each breed. A dog becomes a Champion after winning three CCs under three different judges.

UNITED STATES: The method of achieving Championship status in the USA is based on a points system. In order to become a Champion a dog or bitch must accumulate ten points including two major wins of three points or more under two different judges, in addition to a further point or more from a third judge. The points awarded on any given occasion vary from one to seven depending on the number of dogs and bitches entered.

PREPARING FOR A SHOW

Before you actually enter your dog for a show, it would be a good idea to go along to one as a spectator to see what happens and to see what your dog will be expected to do. Watch the dogs who are being prepared for the ring and you might pick up some tips.

If you have been following the correct grooming procedure, preparation for the show ring should be fairly straightforward. Most Cavalier exhibitors bath their dogs the day before a show to ensure the white markings are thoroughly clean. The Breed Standard requires them to be "pearly" white, and you will be penalised if you use any artifical substance to enhance the colour.

After bathing, your Cavalier will need to be thoroughly groomed. Then, on the day of the show, he should only require brushing and a thorough combing, particularly of the longer parts of the coat, such as the ears and the feathering on the legs and tail. Be sure there are no wet patches around his eyes; wipe around them with dry tissue to remove any traces of tears.

AT THE SHOW

When you arrive at the show, make sure that your dog's details have been correctly entered in the show catalogue. Watch the judging prior to the class you will be taking part in, and note how the judge wants the dogs to be moved in the ring. The judge will probably want the dog to be trotted in a triangle so he has a chance to evaluate the movement going away from him, in profile and coming towards him. Watch the class before yours until it is nearly finished and then you will be ready to collect your dog and go into the ring as the steward calls for the start of your class.

IN THE SHOW RING

All exhibitors wear a number to identify them so you will need a pin to attach this to your coat. In the USA, the dogs are assembled in the order in which they appear in the catalogue but, in the UK, you can choose your own position. When all the dogs in the class are in the ring and have been checked by the steward, the judge will probably walk slowly round the ring having a general look at all the dogs to get an overall impression, and possibly make a mental note of any that particularly please him. Then, it is customary for all the dogs to go around the ring once or twice in an anti-clockwise direction. Hopefully, you will be wearing clothes that do not get in the way, and wearing shoes that will enable you to walk briskly along without losing your balance; avoid high heels and remember that, while you should look smart and tidy, it is the dog who is on show, not you.

The individual assessment comes next, with each dog being placed on the table for examination by the judge. The teeth will be examined to see if the dog has a correct scissor bite (the top teeth closely overlapping the

FACING PAGE: The Cavalier must be trained to pose so that he shows himself off to full advantage.

ABOVE: Success: A combination of careful preparation, training, skilful handling – and a top-quality dog – will lead to honours in the show ring.

bottom teeth). Some practice at home to get him used to this will avoid a struggle on the table. The judge will examine the dog thoroughly from head to tail, and will then ask you to move him. You will have seen the way the other exhibitors have moved their dogs, usually in a triangle, so follow the same pattern. Do this with your dog on a loose lead as, if there is tension, it will interfere with his freedom of movement. At the end of your triangle the judge will be having a last look at the whole dog in profile, so try to keep your Cavalier standing still for the few moments this takes.

When all the dogs in the class have been assessed in this way, the judge will then go around the ring again, picking out the ones that he likes best. The ones not picked out then leave the ring, allowing more space for the potential prize-winners to spread out and look their best for the final decision. The judge may ask some, or all, of these remaining dogs to move across the ring and back, individually, to help him decide on the final placings. He will then pick out the prize-winners, usually the winner first, then the second prize-winner and so on. The class is not considered over until the judge marks down the numbers of the winning dogs in his judging book and sometimes the judge changes his mind at the last minute and switches round two of the exhibits. The prize cards are then given out and, hopefully, there will be applause from the spectators at the ringside.

When all the classes have been judged all the first prize winners, provided they have not subsequently been beaten in another class, enter the ring again and the judge decides on the award for the best of the assembled dogs. If this is an Open Show the overall winner is then declared Best of Breed, if it is a Championship show in the UK he will be awarded the Challenge Certificate. If it is a Championship Show in the USA he will be declared Winners Dog (or Winners Bitch). At Championship Shows there is an award for Reserve to the best male and female, and sometimes the judge calls for the dog or bitch that came second to the winner in its original class to return to the ring for consideration.

At Championship Shows in the UK it is now almost always the case with Cavaliers that males and females are judged by two separate judges as the numbers entered are too great for one judge to cope with. Therefore, when the Challenge Certificate winners have been chosen it is necessary for the two judges to get together to decide between them which is to be Best of Breed and go forward to compete in the Toy Group if it is a Group or All-breed show, or be Best in Show if it is a single breed show. If they are unable to agree, a referee is called in and the referee makes the choice. If there is a Group to compete in, the Best of Breed winner then goes forward to join all the other Toy Best of Breed winners for the Group judge to make his selection; the Group winner then goes forward to compete with the other Group winners for Best in Show.

Chapter Six

BREEDING CAVALIERS

PLANNING A LITTER

It can be very rewarding to breed a litter of puppies from your bitch. You may wish to keep one of the puppies yourself, and the pleasure this will give you, and your bitch, may be considerable. There are always plenty of people who want a Cavalier puppy, so you should be able to find suitable purchasers for the remaining puppies without too much difficulty.

However, there are drawbacks, and you should consider the implications before you embark on breeding from your own bitch. There are a lot of expenses involved: the stud fee which can be considerable, possible travel expenses if the sire you choose lives a long way off, veterinary fees, the cost of extra food and heat for the bitch, the cost of rearing the litter – all these can mount up to quite a considerable sum. There are times when things do not go according to plan; the bitch may miss (i.e. fail to produce any puppies), or she may need to have a caesarean section. The time involved in supervising the pregnant bitch and looking after the puppies is considerable and, while you might enjoy this, it does mean you are not available for other things.

It is a big responsibility to bring puppies into the world when there are so many unwanted pets. It is essential to breed from stock which is free from hereditary defects, but if you were careful to buy your puppy from a reputable breeder, you should not have any problems. Slipping patellas, inguinal hernias, very large umbilical hernias and heart trouble developing at a young age, are all factors which would make any bitch unsuitable to be a mother, as these defects can all be inherited. You may want to produce Cavaliers of a certain colour in your litter. Seek the advice of an experienced breeder who will tell you the likely result of various colour combinations.

THE STUD DOG

If, after careful consideration, you decide you would like to go ahead and breed a litter, the next step is to contact your puppy's breeder. The breeder will be able to confirm that it is advisable to proceed and will probably have some ideas about a suitable stud dog. The male's breeding should be compatible with that of your bitch, and any faults she may have should not be duplicated in the stud dog. The male must be of a good breed type, of sound

FACING PAGE (TOP): It takes many years to establish a successful breeding programme. These Cavaliers are from the Pinerest kennels, USA.
Photo courtesy: Ted and Mary Grace Eubank.

FACING PAGE (BOTTOM): The brood bitch must be a typical specimen of the breed with a sound temperament, and free from inherited conditions.

ABOVE: The stud dog you choose must tie in with your bitch's pedigree, as well as being sound in mind and body.

temperament, and free from any hereditary defects. Most reputable stud dogs are checked for heart and eye conditions, and their owners should have veterinary certificates to confirm there are no problems in these areas. Once you have made your decision, make a booking, advising the stud dog owner of the date your bitch is due in season.

THE BROOD BITCH

You should wait until your bitch is at least eighteen months old before she is bred from, and her last litter should be born before she is eight years old. She should be in excellent condition, carrying just the right amount of weight. Obviously, you are confident that she is of good breed type, of sound temperament, and free from any hereditary defects.

Keep a close eye on your bitch to see exactly when she starts her season. Before the season is due, examine her daily to see if there is any evidence of the vulva starting to swell. Most bitches urinate a lot more frequently as the season approaches. A colourless or creamy discharge may be the first sign of the start of the season and when this turns red, count this as day one. At this stage, inform the stud dog owner so plans can be made for the mating.

For about a week the vulva will continue to swell, and the red discharge may be quite copious. Around the tenth or eleventh day of the season, the vulva becomes softer, although still very enlarged, and the discharge often turns a paler colour. If you gently stroke the side of the vulva, the bitch's tail will swing to the side or up in the air, and this will indicate that she is beginning to 'stand', (which means she is ready for mating). In most cases, the stud dog owner will advise waiting until the following day until a mating is attempted.

THE MATING

The owner of the dog will take control for the mating, but you will be required to keep the bitch on her lead while she is introduced to the dog until the preliminary courtship indicates that she is a willing participant and that he is keen to mate her. Once it is established that she is ready, the owner of the dog will probably ask you to look after her front end, holding her collar while he deals with the actual mating. Maiden bitches can be a bit flighty and sometimes move suddenly at a critical moment.

The dog's penis enters the bitch, and a bulb of tissue then swells inside the vulva. The muscles in the vulva constrict, resulting in the 'tie'. The dog and bitch are now united and until the penis subsides and the vulva muscles relax, they cannot be separated. The tie usually lasts about twenty minutes. When the pair separate, the bitch can then be taken back to the car to sit quietly, while the formalities are completed. The stud fee should be paid immediately on completion of a satisfactory service. Most stud dog owners allow a free service next time the bitch comes in season if no puppies are produced.

PREGNANCY

There will be no physical signs to indicate whether the bitch is in whelp or not until the fifth week, when she may thicken around the waist. Her vulva may remain slightly swollen when the season is over, and if she has a slight, colourless, sticky discharge it is a good sign that she is carrying puppies. Any discharge that is coloured or excessive may require the vet to investigate. Between the 25th and 30th day, the vet will probably be able to tell whether your bitch is in whelp or not.

To begin with, the pregnant bitch's lifestyle should not change radically; she still needs normal exercise, but do not let her jump down from anything two feet high or more. Once you are sure she is pregnant, around 35 days after mating, a calcium and vitamin D compound added to her food will ensure she has adequate supplies of this while the puppies are growing inside her. Lack of calcium may cause eclampsia. This is a potentially fatal condition, which needs immediate treatment by the vet. Around the sixth week, especially if she is getting very heavy round the middle, it is a good idea to divide her food into two meals instead of one large one to avoid any discomfort this may cause. Sometimes the extra pressure on the bladder from the developing puppies makes it necessary for the bitch to urinate during the night.

PREPARATIONS FOR WHELPING

Because you will need to keep a close eye on the bitch before, during and after whelping, you should choose a convenient place which is warm and well-lit for the puppies to be born. Many people use the utility room, which is close at hand, but away from the hustle and bustle of the household. Make sure your bitch gets used to the place you choose, so that she is happy to settle there when whelping commences. If you intend to breed more than one litter, you may choose to obtain a custom-built whelping box but if this is to be a one-off event, a large strong cardboard or plywood box would do. The box should be about 36ins by 24ins and about 28ins high with an open front. There should be something across the front to stop the puppies from falling out. Later on, further adjustment can be made to allow the puppies to enter and leave when required. A ledge around the inside of the box, about three inches from the base, will prevent a puppy from being trapped behind the bitch.

THE WHELPING

The bitch will want to make a nest for her family, and she should be provided with plenty of newspapers to tear up. When she starts to make her nest and is panting spasmodically, whelping is likely to be imminent. Many Cavaliers eat normally prior to whelping, but if your bitch looks disdainfully at her food, this is another sign that the puppies are on the way. Her temperature will have dropped from the normal of 101.5 degrees Fahrenheit to about 99 degrees Fahrenheit. At this stage, wash the bitch's undercarriage with a mild disinfectant, rinse and dry thoroughly, thus ensuring that the teats are clean for the puppies to suckle from. The long hair around her tummy and hindquarters should be clipped to avoid this getting in the way.

The first stage of panting and nest-making may last for some time, and your bitch will appreciate the presence of her trusted owner. The temperature

ABOVE: Most Cavaliers make good mothers and will allow their puppies to suckle even when weaning is well underway.

BELOW: It is a good idea to feed a litter communally, as the competition stimulates their appetite.

ABOVE: As the puppies develop, they become increasingly inquisitive about the outside world.

BELOW: All too soon, the puppies you have reared will be ready to go to new homes.

of the room should be at least 70 degrees Fahrenheit (21 degrees Centigrade), and there should be water available for the bitch to drink if she wants to.

Eventually she will start to have contractions. After a few of these, you will probably see her arch her back, push hard and expel the water bag from her vulva, which will burst, and greenish liquid will soak into the newspaper in her nest. The time between contractions varies, but note when the first contraction occurs, and if regular and purposeful contractions do not produce a puppy within an hour, it would be wise to inform the vet.

Normal procedure usually results in the arrival of a puppy after a few strong contractions. The puppy should be followed by the afterbirth which provides him with oxygen until he is released from the covering membrane and starts to breathe. Instinct should tell the bitch to bite through the cord, release the puppy from its covering membrane, lick its face to encourage breathing, before licking it all over to dry the newborn puppy. It is essential that the puppy is removed at once from its covering membrane so that it can start to breathe.

I always give her a hand at this stage and position the puppy so that we can both have access, rubbing the puppy with a dry towel to ensure it does not get chilled. The afterbirth will follow the puppy and it is perfectly normal for the bitch to eat this. If possible restrict her to two afterbirths as too many may upset her digestive system, although she will benefit from the nourishment they contain. Hopefully,

the puppies will all arrive at reasonable intervals. Between the births, make sure the newborn puppies are feeding from the bitch. Once you think all the puppies have arrived, assistance is needed to take the bitch outside to relieve herself while the whelping box is tidied up. All soiled newspapers should be removed into a bin bag, several layers of clean dry papers put down, and the base of the box should be covered with a large piece of fleece bedding. When the bitch has settled down with her family, offer her some warm milk with honey dissolved in it. Check that all the puppies can suckle, as it is vital that they get a share of the colostrum contained in the first milk, as this gives them protection against infection.

It is advisable to count the afterbirths to see they have all been expelled. In practice, this can be difficult as the bitch sometimes devours them on their way out, so they are not actually seen. However, if she seems unduly restless the day after whelping it may be that she has retained an afterbirth. In this instance, call the vet. An injection will result in the bitch expelling the retained afterbirth. The scenario I have described is what usually happens and is quite straightforward. However, things do not always go according to plan so be prepared to seek advice from an experienced breeder, or call in the vet, should the need arise.

THE NEW MOTHER
For the first 24 hours after the birth, the bitch will benefit from a light diet. She will undoubtedly have eaten some of the afterbirths, which cause black, softish motions, and meals of chicken

and rice will help to restore her digestive system to normal. Drinks of milk, preferably goat's or reconstituted powdered milk with honey or glucose dissolved in it, will ensure she has ample supplies of fluid to produce enough milk. Make sure that clean, fresh water is available at all times. After a few days, the bitch can return to her normal diet, and as the puppies get bigger and are making more demands for greater supplies of milk, her food intake should be stepped up to ensure she does not lose too much condition. Make sure the puppies' nails are trimmed regularly, or they will scratch the bitch while they are feeding.

THE DEVELOPING LITTER
A day or two after birth, the puppies should start to grow and will gain several ounces per week if all is going well. Recording their weights weekly will help you keep a check on this. It is surprising how often a very small or large puppy ends up similar in size to his littermates. The puppies' eyes usually open between twelve and fifteen days, but they do not focus properly for another couple of weeks. Teeth first appear at around twenty-eight days. The pink noses start to go black shortly after birth, but it may take many weeks to finish the process.

WEANING
When the puppies are three to four weeks of age, they are ready to eat a small portion of lean beef, which has been scraped with a sharp spoon, or processed in a food mixer to a paste-like consistency. For the small amount that will be required, it is far better to buy top-quality meat. This should be fed individually to ensure each puppy gets its share. Gently prise open the mouth and press a ball of meat, about the size of a small pea, on the roof of the mouth. This may be rejected once or twice, but as soon as the puppy gets the taste, the meat will disappear rapidly. After several days of placing the meat in the puppy's mouth, it can be offered on a saucer but, again, feed individually. At about four weeks I start the puppies with a milk-type meal. Warm goat's milk is best, with a little honey and half a rusk dissolved in it. If a finger is dipped into the mixture and offered to the puppy to lick, the puppy will quickly learn to feed from a saucer. Once the puppies have a taste for this they can all share a dish together.

When the puppies are eating their milk and meat meals successfully, they should be divided into four meals a day, two of meat and two of milk. Increasingly, they will feed less and less from their mother, and by six weeks they should be fully independent. An alternative to the meat and puppy meal is a complete puppy diet, which can be introduced as soon as a puppy will take some. When weaning a litter, be guided by commonsense. All litters vary, so the guidelines suggested may need to be modified to suit individual requirements.

WORMING
It is now common practice to start worming puppies at three weeks of age, and then fortnightly for their first few weeks. Obtain a suitable wormer from your vet who will advise on dosage and frequency.

Chapter Seven

HEALTH CARE

Many Cavaliers enjoy long, healthy lives with few visits to the vet but, like all pedigree breeds, Cavaliers do have some problems which can crop up with variable frequency. It is the responsibility of the Cavalier owner to keep a check on overall health and condition, and then if a problem occurs, it can be treated in the early stages.

TREATING YOUR DOG AT HOME

Scissors, antiseptic ointment, antiseptic liquid for dilution, and cotton-wool are to be found in most households. In addition to these items, it is useful to keep antihistamine cream and spray, ear and eye drops, kaolin lotion or tablets, and worm tablets. Do not keep antibiotic tablets that have been prescribed for a specific ailment in the hope they will come in handy for something else. Dosing with antibiotics without the advice of a vet can be harmful; these also have a specified life span after which they become ineffective.

A blunt-ended thermometer is a valuable aid to identifying illness. The dog's normal temperature is 101.5 degrees F. (38.5 degrees C.), so 103 degrees and above is considered a raised temperature. The temperature is taken by applying lubricating cream to the thermometer and inserting it into the rectum for one minute, leaving a couple of inches sticking out. A wipe with some tissue will enable the reading to be taken.

VACCINATION

It is normal practice for puppies to be vaccinated against the following killer diseases: distemper, hepatitis, leptospirosis and parvovirus. In some countries, your Cavalier will need to be immunised against rabies. The course of two or three injections, depending on your vet's advice, usually start when your puppy is between 8-12 weeks of age. Your vet will advise you about the procedure but, remember, your Cavalier will not be fully protected until two weeks after the final injection, so keep him in a safe area until then.

The protection your puppy will get from his vaccination programme will need to be reinforced every twelve months. An annual visit to the surgery also allows the vet to examine the dog to ensure no other minor ailments need attention. Should your dog have to go into boarding kennels, proof of vaccination will be required before he is admitted, so keep his card in a safe place where it can be found when needed.

KENNEL COUGH

This is a composite disease consisting of a number of different viruses and bacteria. In some respects it is like the common cold in humans; it is very quickly transmitted from one dog to another in places where a number of dogs are together. Training classes, dog shows and boarding kennels are all possible sources of infection. Because there are so many different germs involved, complete protection by vaccination is not as effective as that given for the other major infectious diseases, although vaccination may prevent the infection from becoming as serious as it might otherwise have been.

Normally, apart from a cough which sounds dreadful, the dog is not adversely affected to any great extent, and the disease runs its course in about a week to ten days. Young puppies and very old dogs are more at risk from this disease and, if the temperature rises, it may be necessary to have a course of antibiotics to shake it off. This disease is extremely infectious and any dog with symptoms of kennel cough should be kept well away from other dogs.

EXTERNAL PARASITES

FLEAS: These can occur in the best regulated households. Hedgehogs, rabbits and cats may introduce them to your Cavalier, quite apart from getting them from other dogs. You may not actually catch sight of a flea, but the tell-tale signs are little black specks in the coat, which will be found when grooming – and your dog will undoubtedly be scratching.

There are numerous remedies for fleas including powder, shampoo and aerosol sprays, many of which are available from pet shops. Quick action is necessary, as fleas breed quickly and lay eggs which can lie dormant for up to a year before they hatch. I use the aerosol spray, which can be obtained from the vet. The spray comes in two separate canisters, one for the dog and one for the carpets, bedding etc., which may be harbouring the eggs. You will probably be able to buy the spray from the vet without the need for an expensive consultation.

LICE: These tiny, grey insects are usually found in the ear flaps. Their whitish eggs may also be seen adhering to the hair. Eradication can be achieved in the same way as fleas. Lice are not common in pet dogs in the UK.

TICKS: These parasites are often found in an area frequented by sheep. They attach themselves to the dog and, from small, brown, tubular-shaped insects, they change as they gorge themselves on the dog's blood, and become round, grey and much bigger, often about a quarter of an inch (6mm) across.

The head is deeply embedded into the skin and can come off and remain in the dog if the person removing the tick is inexperienced. A simple, effective way of ridding the dog of these ugly creatures is to spray them with the insecticidal spray obtained from the vet for fleas, wait half an hour for the spray to have the desired effect. Then, if the tick has not fallen off, remove it with a pair of tweezers. Alcohol applied to the tick can also have the same effect.

EAR MITES: Ear mites cannot easily be seen by the naked eye, but waxy deposits in the ear may indicate their presence, and the dog will scratch at the base of the ear. Drops to eradicate ear mites can be obtained from the vet. If your dog is regularly troubled by this parasite, an application of the appropriate drops on a monthly basis should alleviate the problem. The heavy ears of a Cavalier prevent air circulating freely inside the ear, so inspect them regularly to see that all is well.

CHEYLETIELLA: Sometimes known as 'walking dandruff', this is caused by a tiny insect which transports flakes of skin about the body of the dog. Dandruff-like flakes can be seen in the coat, and the dog will scratch. This insect seems to like Cavaliers particularly, and when large numbers of dogs are kept, it can be a problem to eradicate. A rash on humans can sometimes be caused by these mites. A vet will be able to identify it by examining the affected area with a magnifying glass, or pressing Sellotape on to the dandruff-like flakes and examining them under a microscope. Treatment is usually successful when the dog is bathed, sometimes repeatedly at specific intervals, in a shampoo or wash supplied by the vet.

ECZEMA AND MANGE: It is very unlikely that your Cavalier will be affected by either of these skin disorders. Miscellaneous skin

problems are often erroneously attributed to them. If there is something wrong with the skin which does not clear up within a few days, or if a rash appears on the members of your household, it would be wise to consult the vet.

INTERNAL PARASITES
There are many varieties of parasite which affect all kinds of living creatures, including man. Those most likely to affect dogs are roundworm and tapeworm.

ROUNDWORM: A bitch probably has the larvae of the roundworm in her body tissue in areas which cannot be reached by de-worming compounds. When she becomes pregnant the larvae migrate through the body tissue and find their way into the developing puppies. The larvae hatch out in the puppies' intestines, so the compound to destroy them is then unable to reach the newly-hatched worms through the digestive system. It is therefore highly desirable to eliminate these as early as possible. The first worm treatment should be given at three weeks of age and repeated at fortnightly intervals until the puppy goes for vaccination, when the vet will prescribe a suitable on-going programme.
TAPEWORM: These are not so common as they once were. However, if present, they can undermine the condition of the dog dramatically. Small, rice-like particles are found near the anus; these are dried, discarded sections of the tapeworm's body. The head of the tapeworm is firmly attached to the lining of the dog's intestines and, unless effective

treatment is administered, the worm continues to grow and grow. A remedy supplied by the vet is effective in eradicating tapeworms. As with all medicines, it is important to follow the recommended treatment.

HEARTWORMS: This parasite more commonly affects dogs in the USA and Australia, as the heartworm is transmitted to dogs via the mosquito. Medication can prevent infestation, and should be administered regularly throughout the season when mosquitoes are active, and in some climates it will be needed on a daily basis all through the year.

A-Z OF COMMON AILMENTS

ANAL GLANDS
If your dog keeps dragging his bottom along the ground, many people assume this is because he has worms. In fact, it is far more likely that the anal gland or, more accurately, the anal sac, situated near the anus, has become full and is not emptying naturally. It is quite simple to empty the anal gland. The vet will show you how to do it, so if it requires to be emptied frequently, you will be able to do the job yourself.

BURNS AND SCALDS
Apply cold water to the affected area, which will take out the heat. The coat affords some protection against the skin being damaged by scalds or burns, but keep a careful eye on the damage in case infection sets in. It is necessary for the tissue to be repaired from the inside, so do not apply any medication to the exterior, which will probably only cause dirt to adhere to it, furthering the risk of infection.

DIARRHOEA
This is often caused by over-eating or an inappropriate diet. If your dog is suffering from diarrhoea, do not give any food for twelve hours, but make sure that fresh, drinking water is available. Do not give milk to a dog with diarrhoea as this often makes it worse. Cooked chicken with some boiled rice is an easily digested meal which will help get the digestive system back to normal. Consult the vet if any of the following symptoms are also present: blood in the faeces, vomiting, raised temperature, pain, the dog is very dull and subdued.

EYE DAMAGE
The Cavalier's large eyes sometimes suffer damage if they are scratched by sharp twigs or undergrowth. It can look quite alarming as the front of the eye takes on a bluish, opaque tinge. The eye does not normally contain a network of blood vessels but, when damage occurs, the eye automatically grows some to repair the damaged tissue. It is sometimes possible to see a redness in the eyeball caused by the presence of blood in these repairing vessels. The vet should be consulted to ascertain the extent of the damage and a suitable treatment will be prescribed. Infection can start up in a damaged eye, so antibiotic ointment is often required. The eye will very probably return to normal when the damage heals.

FITS
Some Cavaliers, like many other breeds, occasionally suffer from epileptic or other fits. The dog may

LEFT: Your puppy's vaccination programme should be started when he is between eight and twelve weeks of age.

BELOW: When you groom your dog, check that he is free from external parasites, such as fleas.

ABOVE: The picture of health: It is important to know what a fit dog looks like so that if your Cavalier is off-colour, you will be quick to detect signs of ill health. These Cavaliers, living in New York, USA, are pictured with a Chinese Crested (Powderpuff).

Photo courtesy: Ken Town.

BELOW: Good Companions: The Cavalier is generally a healthy dog, and will, hopefully, experience few major problems during its life.

suddenly pass out; he should be kept warm and quiet until he recovers, which will usually be in a few minutes. When your dog has recovered, take him to your vet, who may be able to prescribe medication. On no account should a Cavalier with this tendency be bred from.

HEART MURMUR

A number of Cavaliers develop a heart murmur by the time they are six years old; this may have little effect on the day-to-day life of a Cavalier. Medication may not be necessary until deterioration in the condition of the heart occurs, and some dogs never require medication. Obviously, occurrence of this condition is being closely monitored, and breeders are being encouraged to screen stock carefully.

HEAT-STROKE

Heat-stroke occurs when the dog's body temperature rises excessively due to being confined somewhere with no access to shade, such as in the back of a car or in a kennel situated in bright sunlight. Even when a car is moving, with the windows open, problems can arise if the sun is shining directly on the dog. A dog suffering from heat-stroke will show signs of discomfort, pant heavily, and may collapse.

It is imperative to bring the temperature down quickly, and this can be done in a variety of ways. Immersion of the dog's torso in a bath, or in a bowl of cold water, will have rapid effect; covering the dog's body in towels soaked with cold water also helps, as does the application of bags of frozen vegetables or ice-cubes to the body. A thermometer will indicate when the temperature has returned to normal. The dog should be moved to a cold area as soon as possible, and kept quiet until recovery is complete. It is advisable to take your dog to the vet to check that he has fully recovered.

STINGS

Antihistamine tablets give rapid relief from stings. These can be useful for stings in the mouth, as Cavaliers often snap at flying insects during the summer. Antihistamine cream can be applied to external stings.

POISONING

Vomiting and sudden collapse may indicate poison has been consumed. This can happen when your Cavalier finds poison that has been put down for rats, foxes, slugs, or other pests. If you are able to identify the type of poison taken, the vet may be able to administer an antidote. If none of the suspect material can be found, a sample of the vomit may help the vet identify the substance. Very speedy action is required or the result may be fatal.

VOMITING

Dogs vomit easily, often from eating rubbish. If the dog seems otherwise normal, starve him for 24 hours, giving only very small drinks of water at regular intervals. After starving, give a small meal of scrambled eggs. Gradually re-introduce the normal diet, but if any of the following signs are also present, consult your vet: diarrhoea, raised temperature, pain, the dog is dull and depressed.

WOUNDS
Minor wounds or grazes usually heal very quickly after initial cleansing with suitably diluted antiseptic. Stick to the manufacturer's recommendations and do not be tempted to make the solution too strong. A deep wound may need to be stitched by the vet.

THE FINAL PARTING
When the time comes for your beloved pet to reach the end of the road, do not delay the sad moment, hoping he will die peacefully in his sleep. If he becomes too ill or disabled to enjoy his life any longer, it is much kinder to take him to the vet, or have the vet come to your home, to allow him the dignity of a painless end, with the comfort and reassurance of your presence in his last moments.

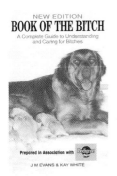

Further Reading for Cavalier owners

Cavalier King Charles Spaniels Today
Sheila Smith
Ringpress Books
Price: £16.99

This outstanding title from the award-winning Book of the Breed series gives you a complete picture of the Cavalier. The author traces the history of the Toy Spaniel from the Royal Courts of Europe to the emergence of the Cavalier as a separate breed some 50 years ago.

There is invauuable advice on caring, training and exercise, showing, judging, breeding and rearing, plus an in-depth analysis of the Breed Standard.
Author Sheila Smith is among the most successful Cavalier breeders of all time.

160 pages. 120 illustrations.

Pet Owner's Guide to Puppy Care & Training
John and Mary Holmes
Ringpress Books
Price: £4.99

Voted Dog Book Of The Year by the Dog Writer's Association of America...a rare award for a British book

The authors draw on a lifetime of experience training dogs for TV and films, obedience competitions and farm work, as well as much-loved pets.
With chapters on Taking On a Puppy, Arriving Home, Family Life, Caring, Health, Understanding, Training and Adolescence, this book will put you on the road to a happy and fulfilling relationship with your dog.

80 pages. 60 colour illustrations.